Lay Ecclesial Ministry

THE STATE OF THE QUESTIONS

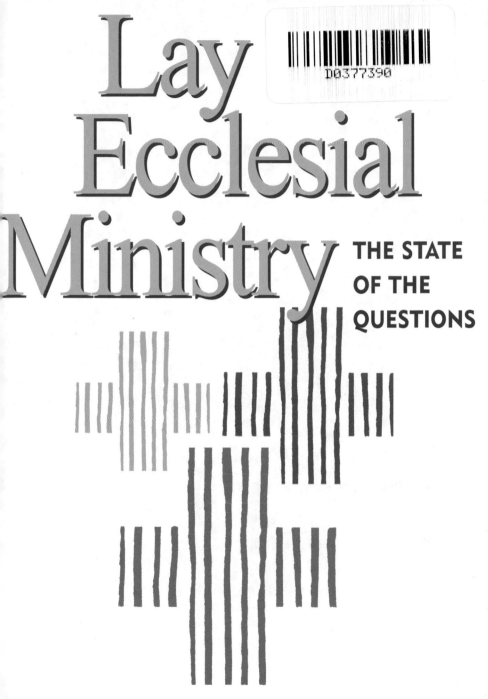

A REPORT OF THE SUBCOMMITTEE ON LAY MINISTRY

COMMITTEE ON THE LAITY
UNITED STATES CONFERENCE OF CATHOLIC BISHOPS
WASHINGTON, D.C.

Lay Ecclesial Ministry: The State of the Questions is a report of the bishops' Subcommittee on Lay Ministry of the Committee on the Laity. It was approved in August 1999 by the members of the Subcommittee and by the members of the Committee on the Laity. It is authorized for publication by the undersigned.

Monsignor Dennis M. Schnurr
General Secretary
NCCB/USCC

First Printing, December 1999
Second Printing, March 2000
Third Printing, January 2002

ISBN 1-57455-345-3

Contents

LIST OF ABBREVIATIONS

DOCUMENTS CITED

AA	*Decree on the Apostolate of the Laity (Apostolicam Actuositatem)*
AG	*Decree on the Church's Missionary Activity (Ad Gentes)*
CL	*The Vocation and Mission of the Lay Faithful in the Church and in the World (Christifideles Laici)*
EA	*The Church in America (Ecclesia in America)*
EN	*On Evangelization in the Modern World (Evangelii Nuntiandi)*
LG	*Dogmatic Constitution on the Church (Lumen Gentium)*
MQ	*On First Tonsure, Minor Orders, and the Subdiaconate (Ministeria Quaedam)*

OTHER ABBREVIATIONS

AGPIM	Association of Graduate Programs in Ministry
CARA	Center for Applied Research in the Apostolate
CCA	USCC Commission on Certification and Accreditation
CELAM	Latin American Bishops Council (Consejo Episcopal Latinoamericano)
CPE	Clinical Pastoral Education programs
FIP	The Federation of Pastoral Institutes (Federación de Institutos Pastorales)
NACPA	National Association of Church Personnel Administrators
NALM	National Association for Lay Ministry
NCCB	National Conference of Catholic Bishops
NCCL	National Conference of Catechetical Leaders
NCWC	National Catholic Welfare Conference
NFCYM	National Federation of Catholic Youth Ministers
RCIA	Rite of Christian Initiation of Adults
USCC	United States Catholic Conference

Introduction

This "state of the questions" report is presented to the National Conference of Catholic Bishops (NCCB) by the Subcommittee on Lay Ministry (Committee on the Laity). For the past four years, the subcommittee has been engaged in a special project known as "Leadership for Lay Ecclesial Ministry." It was supported by a substantial grant from the Lilly Endowment and by conference funds. With this report, the project comes to an end. However, we believe the energy and work generated by this project can and should continue in a variety of ways and at all institutional levels of the Church's life.

Therefore, we offer two things in this report: first, a summary of what we have done and, most importantly, what we have learned; and second, an invitation to determine how the work of this project will be continued so that it serves the need for leadership at a national level as well as the need for practical assistance at local levels.

BACKGROUND

In January 1997, Pope John Paul II addressed a group of French bishops:

> We see a true source of hope in the willingness of a considerable number of lay people to play a more active and diversified role in ecclesial life, and to take the necessary steps to train seriously for this. ("Ad Limina Apostolorum" [January 25, 1997], no. 2, in *L'Osservatore Romano*, February 5, 1997, English edition)

The Holy Father's expression of hope could just as easily and accurately apply to our own country. Over the last two decades, the U.S. Catholic bishops have focused on lay persons serving in church ministries by issuing two pastoral statements and by twice commissioning national research studies about the laity who are responsible for pastoral ministries in parishes. Those efforts together constitute an important foundation and starting point for the current project about which we are reporting.

In 1980, the pastoral statement *Called and Gifted* first recognized and expressed gratitude for a new development since the Second Vatican Council. Lay men and women were responding as volunteers and part-time workers to serve on pastoral councils and other advisory boards and to undertake new roles as special ministers of communion, lectors, catechists, pastoral assistants, and missionaries. The group of laity preparing themselves professionally to work in the Church was given special mention by the bishops, who referred to them as ecclesial ministers. Many of these ecclesial ministers are hired by parishes, diocesan offices, and church agencies to fill staff positions and were entrusted with significant leadership responsibilities. Our project set out to focus specifically on this group of lay ministers. However, we have struggled with the knowledge that the boundaries that distinguish ecclesial ministers from other lay ministers and from all the laity are flexible and permeable; there is no universally accepted delineation.

The first national research study, commissioned by our bishops' conference and published in 1992 as *New Parish Ministers: Laity and Religious on Parish Staffs* (Philip J. Murnion, New York: National Pastoral Life Center), began to measure and describe the extent to which laity were being entrusted with leadership roles in parish ministry. The author, Msgr. Philip J. Murnion, estimated that in parish ministry alone 21,500 lay persons (including vowed religious) worked full- or part-time in formal pastoral roles (as distinct from support staff and maintenance roles). This number did not include parochial school faculties, which had been studied by other groups. A follow-up study entitled *Parishes and Parish Ministers* (Philip J. Murnion and David DeLambo, New York: National Pastoral Life Center, 1999) now estimates that this same group of lay ministers has grown to 29,145—an increase of 35 percent. The study also showed that 60 percent of U.S. parishes employ lay ministers. These lay ministers can also be found in hospitals and health care institutions, educational institutions, prisons, seaports, and airports. In 1996, at least 3,500 such individuals carried on the ministry of the Church in those settings.

In 1995, the NCCB issued a second pastoral statement on the laity entitled *Called and Gifted for the Third Millennium* (Washington, D.C.: United States Catholic Conference). In this document, the bishops provided a more complete description of lay ministries and used the category of "ecclesial lay minister" to identify a wide variety of people who bring their gifts and talents to serve the Church and who function under the aegis or authorization of the Church.

Noting that lay ministry continues to develop in practice and in theology, in this 1995 pastoral statement, the bishops pledged to "expand our study and dialogue concerning lay ministry in order to understand better the critical issues and find effective ways to address them. The new evangelization will become a reality only if ordained and lay members of Christ's faithful understand their roles and ministries as complementary, and their purposes joined to the one mission and ministry of Jesus Christ" (p. 18).

To address this commitment specifically, the NCCB Committee on the Laity established the Subcommittee on Lay Ministry, whose purpose was to come to a better understanding of the range of issues concerning lay ministry in the Church in the United States; given a deepened understanding of them, to bring certain issues to the attention of the episcopal conference; and to offer options for addressing them.

LEADERSHIP FOR LAY ECCLESIAL MINISTRY PROJECT

In 1995, the subcommittee designed and undertook the Leadership for Lay Ecclesial Ministry Project. The project, which was supported by a grant from the Lilly Endowment, had three goals:

(1) To provide diocesan bishops and their collaborators/advisors with information and other forms of assistance in order for them to understand the scope and implications of the phenomenon of lay ecclesial ministry for dioceses in the U.S. and to sharpen their abilities for leadership, especially in the areas of policy development and pastoral practice regarding lay ecclesial ministry in a diocese, for example, formation and education, placement, evaluation, accountability, credentialing, certification, ministerial collaboration, and theological and canonical considerations

(2) To stimulate conversation and collaboration among a variety of national ministerial groups, lay formation programs, and institutions of higher education about ensuring that high quality pastoral ministry always be provided to the Church and about the distinct place of professionally prepared lay ministers in this context

(3) To propose to the bishops' conference a longer-range plan for how it might exercise leadership for lay ecclesial ministry

This project has been for us, the members and advisors of the subcommittee, an extensive and valuable experience of learning through listening, discussion, and reflection. The process has included bishops, theologians, canonists, priests, deacons, lay ministers, educators, diocesan and parish staff, representatives of various cultural and ethnic communities, and representatives from the episcopal conferences of Latin America and Canada. During the past four years, we have paid attention in a sustained and systematic way to a "new thing" that we believe the Holy Spirit has been creating in the Catholic Church in the United States. We have tried to understand the phenomenon of lay ecclesial ministry from different perspectives and with a variety of methods. We have interpreted the various data and have reached conclusions that represent our best—though tentative—reading of a reality that is still developing and will need continued guidance. This process of discernment has led us to propose possible actions, as well as to identify areas needing more attention, understanding, judgment, and decision. Our "state of the questions" report integrates and reflects work associated with a process of discerning that needs to be carried out at each stage.

Our subcommittee organized its work around the priority concerns of the bishops, priorities that were determined by surveying all the bishops at the beginning of the project. We also surveyed diocesan staff, graduate programs in ministry, and associations of lay ministers. After the survey phase was completed, we conducted five focus groups of bishops in different regions of the country. The focus groups supplemented the survey information and helped us to sharpen our appreciation of the issues of lay ecclesial ministry that were ranked in the surveys as most important. We found that all those surveyed and consulted agreed that the following six areas were of greatest interest and concern:

* The term "lay minister"
* A theology of lay ministry
* The formation of lay ministers
* The relationship between lay ministers and ordained ministers
* The financial and human resources issues connected with lay ministry
* The multicultural issues connected with lay ministry

Our report treats each topic separately, beginning with our conclusions and proposals, which are offered for further dialogue and refinement. The conclusions and proposals are followed by the findings that led us to those conclusions as well as a review of what we learned from the surveys, focus groups, and subcommittee activities. We believe that these conclusions and proposals warrant further study.

At the conclusion of *Parishes and Parish Ministers*, an important observation is made:

> It appears that the practice of pastoral ministry that led to engaging more and more laypeople in parish ministry outstrips the theology and church policy regarding lay ministry. This is to be expected. In fact, it is beneficial that the practice has a chance to develop before it is codified too tightly. Nonetheless, the need to continue theological reflection, ministerial clarification, and church policy development is evident if we are to make the most of the gifts to the church represented by these parish ministers and provide the kind of support for them and their pastors to foster appropriate and effective collaboration. (p. 74)

We strongly concur with this viewpoint and, in the following sections of our report, we hope not only to elaborate on the state of these questions, but also—with the involvement and support of the U.S. bishops—to move the questions themselves to new levels of awareness, commitment, and action.

The Term "Lay Ecclesial Minister"

I. CONCLUSIONS FROM THE SUBCOMMITTEE

CONCLUSION 1: For several reasons, the subcommittee prefers the term "lay ecclesial minister" for the group of ministers that have been the focus of this project. First, the word "lay" underscores the fact that persons in this group remain first, foremost, and always members of the laity. Their work is a specific and legitimate expression of the general vocation of all lay persons. When we use the term "lay ecclesial minister," we do not refer to all those who minister in response to their baptism within the church community or the world; the word "ecclesial" denotes not only that the ministry of these lay persons has a place within the communion of the Church but also that it is to be submitted to the judgment and supervision of the hierarchy. It is not simply an activity undertaken on personal initiative. Finally, the subcommittee regards the entire term "lay ecclesial minister" as identifying a broad category. It is not a specific job title. Lay ecclesial minister is a generic term. We use it to establish a framework to indicate what is common to many roles and responsibilities undertaken by lay persons, for example, director of religious education, pastoral associate, youth minister, campus chaplain, hospital chaplain, and director of RCIA.

CONCLUSION 2: Identity as a lay ecclesial minister is partly a question of personal awareness and intentionality and partly a matter of recognition by official church authority. The two dimensions must converge. In our project and in this report, "lay ecclesial minister" has come to mean the following:

- A fully initiated lay member of the Christian faithful (including vowed religious) who is responding to the empowerment and gifts of the Holy Spirit received in baptism and confirmation, which enable one to share in some form of ministry
- One who responds to a call or invitation to participate in ministry and who has prepared through a process of prayerful discernment
- One who has received the necessary formation, education, and training to function competently within the given area of ministry
- One who intentionally brings personal competencies and gifts to serve the Church's mission through a specific ministry of ecclesial leadership and who does so with community recognition and support
- One to whom a formal and public role in ministry has been entrusted or upon whom an office has been conferred by competent ecclesiastical authority
- One who has been installed in a ministry through the authority of the bishop or his representative, perhaps using a public ritual
- One who commits to performing the duties of a ministry in a stable manner
- A paid staff person (full- or part-time) or a volunteer who has responsibility and the necessary authority for institutional leadership in a particular area of ministry

We propose that the characteristics enumerated above depict our vision of the lay ecclesial minister; in other words, it is highly desirable that each of them be present to some degree in every minister. We do not consider it our responsibility to develop an exhaustive list of persons who fit into the category of "lay ecclesial minister." The needs of the local church as well as the perspective and authority of its diocesan bishop are essential to determining this.

II. BACKGROUND FOR SUBCOMMITTEE CONCLUSIONS
A. Subcommittee Findings

In the post-conciliar period, a distinctly new and different group of lay ministers has emerged in the Church in the United States. This group consists of lay women and men performing roles that entail varying degrees of pastoral leadership and administration in parishes, church agencies, and organizations, and at diocesan and national levels. They are doing so in a public, stable, recognized, and authorized manner. Furthermore, when these lay ministers speak of their responsibilities, they emphasize ministering in ways that are distinguished from, yet complementary to, the roles of ordained ministers. Many of them also express a deep sense of vocation that is part of their personal identity and that motivates what they are doing. Many have sought academic credentials and diocesan certification in order to prepare for their ministry.

Research on lay ministry conducted for the bishops' conference by the National Pastoral Life Center in 1992 and 1999 focused in considerable detail on the members of this group who serve in parish positions. In their two pastoral statements on the laity (*Called and Gifted* and *Called and Gifted for the Third Millennium*), the U.S. bishops referred to these persons, whether in parish, diocesan, or other institutional positions, using the term "ecclesial minister." The existence and legitimacy of this type of lay ministry is expressed in documents of the Universal Church ranging from the Second Vatican Council's *Apostolicam Actuositatem* (AA), no. 22, to Pope John Paul II's *Christifideles Laici* (CL), no. 23, to the *Code of Canon Law* (cc. 228-31), to Pope John Paul II's apostolic exhortation *Ecclesia in America* (EA), no. 44.

From the beginning, the subcommittee intended to focus narrowly and sharply on this particular group of lay ministers in order to understand their needs, to reflect on their relationship with ordained ministers, and to assess how they are shaping pastoral ministry, especially at the parish level by the very fact of their expanding participation in it. At the basis of our concern for lay ecclesial ministry is (a) the conviction that these ministers are a necessary part of the public ministry of the Church and (b) a desire to ensure that their roles are developed and related to the ministry of the ordained in such a way that all the faithful receive the best possible pastoral care.

In addition to acknowledging the emergence of this distinct group of lay ministers, the subcommittee also acknowledges that this specific group of laity in ecclesial ministries represents but one way in which lay people respond to the call to participate more fully in the mission of the Church and to collaborate with others in accomplishing it. This group of lay ministers exists in a larger context of church ministry and lay participation. The larger context represents territory that needs to be mapped if there is to be a proper understanding of the roles and responsibilities of lay ecclesial ministers. Yet when one attempts to do this mapping, it quickly becomes apparent how fluid is the picture and how permeable are the boundaries between different groups of laity. As yet there is no single, definitive way to categorize and distinguish the many ways in which lay persons are participating and collaborating in the Church's life and mission. The spectrum of activity is broad.

Many questions arise. For example, how is the limited group of lay ecclesial ministers to be distinguished from a larger group of laity who undertake—on a volunteer and periodic basis—certain church ministries, such as reader, catechist, and special minister of communion? How is the group of lay persons who minister in direct service to the Church to be distinguished from, and yet related to, all other laity who participate in the mission of the Church? As distinctions are made, how is it possible to recognize that the same lay person can simultaneously be in several groups depending upon the circumstances?

In an attempt to achieve focus and direction, the subcommittee began this project with its own working definition of the lay ecclesial minister: professionally prepared men and women, including vowed religious, who are in positions of service and leadership in the Church.

While focusing on lay ministers in stable, public, authorized roles of leadership, the subcommittee reached the end of the project with a new understanding of the context in which these lay persons are present and with an expanded list of elements to describe them. By doing what can be described as "clearing away the underbrush," we think we have laid out a path for study and dialogue by theologians, church leaders, and lay ministers themselves.

Early in the project, the limitations of our working definition became apparent. While the use of "professional" can be helpful insofar as it denotes "prepared" or "qualified," the term can also be problematic to the extent that it connotes elitism and privilege. There was concern that the definition excluded volunteers who might be exercising significant roles of leadership and might even be considered de facto staff, but who were not on the payroll. This is an especially sensitive issue within some of the ethnic communities. Finally, this definition did not seem to disclose enough about the conditions under which persons would legitimately enter and remain in positions of service and leadership.

In light of these and other learning experiences, the members of the subcommittee decided not to propose a formal definition, but rather to offer the descriptive elements we think are essential for delineating the group of laity who are in public roles of pastoral responsibility and leadership. The descriptive elements we have chosen for the lay ecclesial minister are a result of our theological reflection, our study of teaching documents of the Church, our consultation with lay ministers and theologians, and our interpretation of the empirical information available in research and other studies. In our judgment, it is this specific group of lay ecclesial ministers that needs our continuing systematic attention if we bishops are to be good stewards of this gift to the Church and to blend their ministries with those of the ordained into a unity of service and mission.

B. What We Learned from Bishops' Surveys and Focus Groups

Defining the term "lay minister" was not included as an issue in the survey to which the bishops responded. Many of them, however, commented on the limitations of the working definition that the subcommittee had used. Several comments mentioned the need for clarification of the distinction between ecclesial ministry and universal service. One asked if ministry depends on official designation and, if so, how that designation should be granted. A few asked that the differences between ordained ministry (particularly diaconal) and lay ministry be addressed. Another referred to the confusion that results because "ministry is being used in so many senses."

Similar concerns about the working definition were mentioned in the focus groups. Several groups commented that using the term "ministry" for the volunteers at bingo or for basketball or soccer coaches creates misunderstandings. The focus groups also emphasized the need to distinguish ecclesial ministry without neglecting the ministry of the laity in transforming the world. Some groups cautioned against creating "a new separation based on degree" and the exclusion of charismatic volunteer leaders from the definition.

C. What We Learned from Subcommittee Activities

The question of who belongs in the category of lay ecclesial ministers was a thread running through all the subcommittee activities. It received specific attention during the theological colloquium, particularly during a general discussion in which participants struggled with the differences between the general call to ministry, which is given to all the baptized, and the more specific call to ecclesial ministry. The issue was discussed, and the thinking of the subcommittee was shaped at least in part by the lay ecclesial ministers themselves, who met representing their ministerial associations and their ethnic communities. We learned from them the importance of working toward a description of lay ecclesial ministers; of striving for clarity in titles, roles, and expectations since all of these affect collaboration; and of recognizing the role of volunteers.

Toward a Theology of Lay Ecclesial Ministry

I. CONCLUSIONS AND PROPOSAL FROM THE SUBCOMMITTEE

Lay ecclesial ministry is, in many ways, a new phenomenon for our Church. Thus, these conclusions on the theology of lay ecclesial ministry are offered not as the final word, but as a faithful beginning. They are not meant to represent a comprehensive theology, but rather a starting point for discussion.

A. The Foundations for Lay Ecclesial Ministry

CONCLUSION 1: One's understanding of ecclesiology affects one's understanding of ministry. An appreciation of the mission of the Church is essential when speaking about all ministry, including lay ecclesial ministry. The Church, as sign and instrument, continues the mission of Christ, which is directed toward the salvation of humanity and the transformation of the world. Mission is accomplished in communion (*communio*), which recognizes an equality of persons and a differentiation of roles (cf. CL, no. 52; AA, no. 10).

CONCLUSION 2: All ministry serves this mission. The baptized serve this mission and share in Christ's priestly, prophetic, and royal office (cf. c. 204.1; LG, no. 31).

CONCLUSION 3: Lay ecclesial ministry is rooted in and flows from the sacraments of initiation, which incorporate indi-

14

viduals into the body of Christ and call them to mission (cf. LG, nos. 31, 33; AA, nos. 2, 3; CL, no. 23).

CONCLUSION 4: Special charisms of the Holy Spirit, which flow from the sacraments of initiation, equip lay ecclesial ministers for their special tasks within the Church (cf. LG, no. 12; AA, no. 3; Rom 12:3-8; 1 Cor 12:4-11; Eph 4:7-13).

B. Lay Ecclesial Ministers as Laity

CONCLUSION 5: The whole Church is missionary. All of the faithful, including the laity, by virtue of their baptism and confirmation, are given a share in Christ's priestly ministry. Such ministry is appropriate in its own right and should not be seen as a way of participating in the ministry of the ordained (cf. AG, no. 2; LG, no. 31).

CONCLUSION 6: One element of the unique character of the laity, within the one mission of the Church, is its secular character. Because of this secular character, the laity are the Church in the heart of the world and bring the world into the heart of the Church. The laity's missionary activity in the world is sometimes referred to as an apostolate (cf. LG, nos. 31, 33; AA, no. 2; CL, no. 15).

CONCLUSION 7: All of the laity are called to work toward the transformation of the secular world. Some do this by working in the secular realm; others do this by working in the Church and focusing on the building of ecclesial communion, which has as its ultimate purpose the transformation of the world. Lay ecclesial ministry should not be seen as a retreat by the laity from their role in the secular realm. Rather lay ecclesial ministry is an affirmation that the Spirit can call the lay faithful to participation in the building of the Church in various ways (cf. LG, no. 12; EA, no. 44).

C. Lay Ecclesial Ministers as Ecclesial Ministers

CONCLUSION 8: Some, whom we are naming lay ecclesial ministers, are called to a ministry within the Church as a further specification and application of what all laity are called and equipped to do. This group of laity can be distinguished from the general body of all the lay faithful, not by reason of merit or rank, but by reason of a call to service made possible by certain gifts of the Holy Spirit, by the generous response of the person, and by an act of authorizing and sending by the proper ecclesiastical authority (cf. Lk 10:1).

CONCLUSION 9: The use of the term "lay ecclesial ministers" for this group shows the following: first, that the immediate reference point of their ministry is the church community itself and, second, that their ministry is exercised not solely on their own initiative, but as a publicly recognized and authorized action within a particular ecclesial community.

CONCLUSION 10: The majority of lay ecclesial ministers carry out duties and responsibilities that can be considered proper to the laity. Examples of these ministries might include music director, director of religious education, youth minister, social justice director, business manager, bereavement ministry coordinator, and principal of a Catholic school. As with all qualified lay persons, some ecclesial ministers may be called to fulfill those ecclesiastical offices that are open to them in the law (c. 228). A small percentage of lay ecclesial ministers, however, serve in ministries that are proper to the ordained (cf. c. 517.2, on administering the pastoral life of a parish). A few positions, such as pastoral associate, sometimes combine responsibilities proper to the laity and responsibilities proper to the ordained.

CONCLUSION 11: By virtue of the charisms received from the Spirit, lay ecclesial ministers have the right and duty to apply their gifts for the mission of the Church. It is important that the unique gifts, expertise, and insights of lay ecclesial ministers be fully incorporated into the life of the Church, in communion with the pastors of the Church (cf. AA, no. 3; LG, no. 12; c. 225).

CONCLUSION 12: The diverse gifts of the laity, who represent many cultures, are a blessing to our Church and are vital to fulfilling the Church's mission. Each individual culture contributes through its special gifts to the good of the other cultures and of the whole Church. Our Church is impoverished when the gifts of diverse cultures are not present within those designated as lay ecclesial ministers (cf. LG, no. 13).

D. The Role of Lay Ecclesial Ministers in Relation to Ordained Ministers

CONCLUSION 13: Lay ecclesial ministry and the ministry of the ordained complement each other within the dynamic *communio* of the Church. They are not in competition. While the phenomenon of lay ecclesial ministry arose during a time of decline in priestly vocations in certain parts of the world, it should not be seen simply as an emergency response. Each expression of ministry is needed in its full dignity and strength if the Church is to be fully alive in its communion and mission (cf. LG, no. 10; CL, no. 20; EA, no. 39).

CONCLUSION 14: Lay ecclesial ministry can be understood as a response to a call from God to work alongside ordained ministers in the service of and within the ecclesial community. Ordained ministers are to acknowledge and to promote the mission of all persons, including the service of lay ecclesial ministers in the Church and in the world (cf. EN, no. 73; cf. c. 275.2).

CONCLUSION 15: Effective collaboration requires a recognition of the basic equality of persons, as well as a necessary distinction or differentiation in their roles and responsibilities. The ordained and the laity share in the one ministry of Christ and, in their distinctive roles, work toward accomplishing the one mission that Christ has given the Church (cf. EA, no. 39; LG, no. 10).

CONCLUSION 16: To speak of a genuine collaboration of ordained ministers and lay ecclesial ministers diminishes neither the sacramental character of ordination nor the properly secular character of the laity, but rather enriches both.

E. The Role of Bishops in Relation to Lay Ecclesial Ministers

CONCLUSION 17: As a group of diverse ministries within the Church, lay ecclesial ministry is part of the work of the local church. It is important for bishops to foster and to guide the use of the gifts that lay ecclesial ministers bring, "not [to] extinguish the Spirit . . . [but to] test everything [and] retain what is good" (1 Thes 5:19; cf. 1 Thes 5:12, 21; AA, no. 3; LG, no. 12).

CONCLUSION 18: One of the roles of the local bishop is to maintain the dynamic *communio* of vocations within the diocese by helping to discern and to encourage all vocations, by fostering collaboration, and by acting as a center of unity.

CONCLUSION 19: Bishops have the responsibility to see that lay ecclesial ministers in their dioceses are properly qualified, have received the necessary formation and education, and continue to receive ongoing formation and education for the benefit of the local church (cf. c. 231; EA, no. 44).

CONCLUSION 20: One of the responsibilities for bishops remains to affirm the distinctive character of lay ecclesial ministry so that its validity as a form of service within the Church can be recognized by all (EA, no. 44).

CONCLUSION 21: Lay ecclesial ministers serve in the name of the Church. Most of the tasks undertaken by them are proper to the laity and, sometimes, other tasks belong properly to the ordained (e.g., celebrating baptisms, witnessing marriages). The language of "delegation" is preferred for tasks that belong properly to the ordained. However, if this language of delegation is used for all tasks undertaken by lay ecclesial ministers, there is a risk of subsuming all lay mission and ministry into the office of the ordained. Also, there is a risk that the ministry and mission of the laity could lose their distinctive characteristics. The recommended language for the majority of lay ecclesial ministry, which does belong properly to the laity, includes "entrusting," "commissioning," or "instituting." In addition, the language of "conferring offices" or "installing" can also be used in some of these cases that are proper to the laity, as well as in cases where a lay ecclesial minister is delegated tasks that are proper to the ordained (MQ).

CONCLUSION 22: Throughout the history of the Church, the hierarchy has been responsible for ordering its ministries. The official ministries vary in response to needs that change over time. Examples of changes in ministries include the following: the creation of minor orders such as porter, lector, exorcist, and acolyte; the creation of the major order subdeacon; the subsequent suppression of porter, exorcist, and subdeacon; and the preservation of lector and acolyte as installed ministries rather than as minor orders. Bishops should continue to be attentive to the needs of faith communities when considering desired ministries.

CONCLUSION 23: The emerging reality of lay ecclesial ministry now needs the attention of the bishops and their leadership in structuring these ministries in fidelity to apostolic tradition and in response to the needs of the community. The Holy Spirit freely bestows gifts on all the faithful, empowering them to respond to a call to ministry. When ordering ministries, church authority has the responsibility to structure and to order its ministries both in faithfulness to the apostolic tradition and in response to the community's needs at a given time in history. These dynamics of structuring and ordering and the empowerment with gifts are occurring now as we do our part to provide for the future of lay ecclesial ministry.

CONCLUSION 24: In general, lay ecclesial ministers should be designated by the diocesan bishop (or representative) to their ministerial assignments within the diocese.

F. The Experience of Lay Ecclesial Ministry

CONCLUSION 25: Lay ecclesial ministry is a gift of the Spirit to the Church. The experience of the past thirty-five years can be seen as the grace-filled work of the Spirit.

CONCLUSION 26: Lay ecclesial ministry is experienced by many to be a call to ministry, a vocation. It is the role and responsibility of the entire Church (including the bishop and the local parish community) to foster, nurture, encourage, and help discern all vocations to ministry.

CONCLUSION 27: The contemporary lived experience of lay ecclesial ministry highlights the fact that any discussion of the role of the laity in the life of the Church has to balance fidelity to Scripture and Tradition with the charismatic activity of the Spirit. Such discussion must, at the same time, be both bold and faithful.

CONCLUSION 28: Inasmuch as realities can be quite different, attending to the theology and practice of lay ecclesial ministry in other countries is important for our own development of the theology of lay ecclesial ministry.

PROPOSAL TO BE CONSIDERED BY BISHOPS

That the conference make provision within its committee structure to continue to promote and to share the results of the following:

(1) Dialogue among bishops, theologians, canonists, ordained ministers, and lay ecclesial ministers for the further articulation of the theology of lay ecclesial ministry.

(2) Scholarly research and writing about the theology of ministry, including such aspects as ministry rooted in the sacraments of initiation as well as in the gifts of the Spirit, the relationship between baptism and orders, and the lay vocation to ministry.

II. BACKGROUND FOR SUBCOMMITTEE CONCLUSIONS AND PROPOSAL

A. Subcommittee Findings

The theology of lay ecclesial ministry is in a phase of ongoing development. The conclusions listed are a result of the subcommittee's work these last four years. These conclusions do not propose a complete, comprehensive theology; rather, they are the fruits of our learning. The conclusions are grounded in our tradition, and they are Spirit-centered. They reflect an ecclesiology that recognizes the Church as missionary. In *Lumen Gentium*, the council fathers speak of the Holy Spirit distributing special graces among the faithful, making them fit and ready to undertake the various tasks or offices needed for the renewal and building of the Church (no. 12). We believe that lay ecclesial ministry, as a whole, is a grace of the Spirit.

B. What We Learned from Bishops' Surveys and Focus Groups

Bishops responding to the initial survey identified the theology of lay ministry as one of the top issues needing priority attention during this project. Several bishops included additional comments, such as the following: "I would like to see a developed ecclesiology that includes the development of lay ministry"; "[The] issue of ecclesiology as understood and enunciated by the magisterium is crucial to a competent, harmonious, and professional exercise of lay ministry"; "This study could be very destructive if it . . . encourages anti-clerical sentiment"; "[My hopes are that this project address] the vision of [the] Second Vatican Council for lay ministry"; "[The study should foster] openness in the Church in discussing issues of concern for lay ministers, for example, women in the church, collegiality, discrimination, justice in the church, polarization"; and "A proper theological basis for lay ministry is essential and would by necessity address the other issues."

The need for further theological reflection on lay ministry was also expressed during the focus groups. One group noted that the development of such a theology should be based on an ecclesiology that arises from Christology and sacramental theology. Viewing lay ministry as a function or profession is based on an incorrect assumption. Some of the focus group participants further commented that an examination of missiology would be helpful in developing the understanding of how Christ "sends" ministers. Another group saw the underlying ecclesiology for lay ministry as the most important issue. They observed that clearer definitions, descriptions, or delineations would help bishops and pastors. Still another group agreed that developing a theology of lay ministry is most important, noting the long process of clarification that continues around the use of the word "ministry." Other focus group participants commented that it would be helpful to clarify the distinction between the vocation of the Christian in the world and in ministry. They also noted that there are different ecclesiologies that exist within the diocese and parish.

C. What We Learned from Subcommittee Activities

Theological Colloquium

In May 1997, the subcommittee sponsored a theological colloquium "Toward a Theology of Ecclesial Lay Ministry" at the University of Dayton. A steering committee, which included bishops and theologians, planned the colloquium and modeled the spirit of discernment and collaboration that characterized the colloquium itself. The subcommittee invited bishops who had doctoral degrees in theology or canon law to join other theologians and canonists in the discussion of nine papers that were commissioned for the colloquium. (The papers were published in 1998 by the United States Catholic Conference [USCC] as *Together in God's Service: Toward a Theology of Ecclesial Lay Ministry* [to order, call 800-235-8722].) The forty-six participants included bishops, priests, religious, and lay men and women. The goals for the colloquium were to begin to articulate a theology of lay ministry, to make proposals to the subcommittee for further activity, and to model how bishops and theologians can come together for theological discussion. Evaluations by the participants indicated that, although the time was limited, the colloquium accomplished its goals.

Development of a Working Paper on the Theology of Lay Ecclesial Ministry

The consensus statements that emerged from the colloquium discussions became the basis for continued reflection by the subcommittee and others. Members of the subcommittee wrote, reviewed, and revised a working paper on the theology of lay ecclesial ministry.

Their work was supplemented by that of theologians and canonists who served as consultants. The working paper led to the development of the conclusions presented in this report.

Workshop for Bishops

In November 1997, the subcommittee sponsored a bishops' workshop before the NCCB/USCC general meeting. More than seventy bishops participated and, in addition to other topics, engaged in discussion of the working paper on the theology of lay ministry, a discussion stimulated by the presentations of Archbishop Daniel E. Pilarczyk and Dr. Monika K. Hellwig. Evaluations of the workshop indicated that the bishops had a strong desire for continued theological reflection and discussion on lay ecclesial ministry.

Gatherings of Ministers

In September 1997, the subcommittee met with twenty-two representatives of professional ministerial associations, and in March 1998, with seventeen representatives of ten different "minority" ethnic communities. Both groups reviewed parts of the working paper, particularly the definition or description of lay ecclesial ministers. Their experiences and insights contributed to the continued development of the subcommittee's work on the theology of lay ecclesial ministry.

Preparation of Lay Ecclesial Ministers

I. CONCLUSIONS AND PROPOSALS FROM THE SUBCOMMITTEE

CONCLUSION 1: The statement in *Ecclesia in America* that "intra-ecclesial" work by laity "should be undertaken only by men and women who have received the necessary training in accordance with clearly defined criteria" (no. 44) echoes the words of canon 231 that "lay persons who devote themselves permanently or temporarily to some special service of the Church are obliged to acquire the appropriate formation which is required to fulfill their function properly." We share this concern about ensuring the quality of the preparation of lay ecclesial ministers.

A growing number of dioceses have developed their own standards and certification processes for different lay ministry positions. Such standards are valuable in the screening and placement of lay ministers. We have also noted the growing movement toward the creation of standards by national ministerial groups themselves, standards that have subsequently been approved by our USCC Commission on Certification and Accreditation (CCA). These standards are also used by ministry formation programs, both diocesan and university-based, as one resource in curriculum construction and revision.

CONCLUSION 2: Not every formation program is suited or adequate for the preparation of every lay minister. We conclude that dialogue among the various agencies (diocesan lay ministry formation programs, seminaries, university-based programs) would be helpful to ensure the best use of resources and the provision of quality programs for prospective lay ministers. There is a leadership role for the diocesan bishop or the bishops of a province or region in promoting such dialogue.

The growth in the number of ministry formation programs, both diocesan and university-based, testifies to the growth in the number of those wishing to prepare for ministry and the resourcefulness of the dioceses and academic institutions. Such growth may be helpful for meeting the needs of the Church, or it may unnecessarily duplicate or overextend already existing resources.

CONCLUSION 3:   Lay ministers have themselves expressed their need for continuing education. We agree that it is needed by all engaged in ministry. We recognize that there will be occasions when laity, religious, deacons, and priests need to address issues unique to their state in life and the implications of those issues for their ministry. We also believe that jointly experiencing formation and continuing education, as well as formation courses and workshops, can help build the relationships that are key to collaboration in ministry. Both approaches have been used successfully and deserve support.

CONCLUSION 4:   In most diocesan formation programs, the costs are usually shared by the diocese, the parish, and the student. While some graduate schools give generous assistance—drawn from limited institutional funds—to lay students preparing for ministry, many graduate students assume full responsibility for the costs of their preparation (preparation for a ministry that does not offer large compensation packages). Some dioceses have established scholarship programs specifically for lay ministers. We believe that such programs should be encouraged, as well as programs that help poorer parishes to educate their leaders who are often members of minority groups.

CONCLUSION 5:   Lay ministers speak often and reverently of their call or vocation to ministry, a call that finds its origin in the call of God and its confirmation in the appointment to a specific ministry within the Church. These ministers often experience such a call within, and sometimes transcending, a vocation to married, single, or religious life. The Church has not spoken of lay ministry as a vocation beyond the words in *Called and Gifted for the Third Millennium*: "Ecclesial lay ministers speak of their work, their service, as a calling, not merely a job. They believe God has called them to their ministry, and often the parish priest is the means of discerning the call" (p. 17). We conclude that this call or vocation is worthy of respect and sustained attention.

PROPOSALS TO BE CONSIDERED BY BISHOPS

(1) That the conference offer guidance for the preparation of lay ecclesial ministers. That guidance would be developed from existing resources (e.g., nationally approved standards) and experiences (diocesan ministry formation and graduate programs in ministry) and could be applied according to local situations and circumstances. The guidance could be in the form of a handbook similar to the directory being prepared for deacons, although it would not have the force of particular law.

(2) That the conference facilitate dialogue among the various institutions involved with the formation of lay ecclesial ministers, with the goal of ensuring the best use of resources and the provision of quality programs for prospective lay ministers.

II. BACKGROUND FOR SUBCOMMITTEE CONCLUSIONS AND PROPOSALS

A. Subcommittee Findings

The path to lay ecclesial ministry begins with the inspiration of God. For those in parish ministry, that inspiration may be in the form of an invitation by the pastor or some member of the parish staff to consider ministry or it may be the stirrings of the heart that are later affirmed by others on the parish staff or within the parish community. For other ministries, it is similar. Campus chaplains, for example, are frequently the ones who encourage students, particularly students who sense a desire for more involvement with the Church, to consider campus ministry.

In a very real sense, ministers are called by God and by the church community. Responding to that call leads one to prepare seriously for the ministry. The larger society in which we live and minister is one that asks credentials of all who would serve it. The development of competencies and the acquisition of degrees do not substitute for the charism or call to ministry, but they are usually an essential complement to that call.

Elements of Preparation

The preparation of lay ecclesial ministers includes several elements. The first element, spiritual formation, is key, and this is accomplished in several ways: group theological reflection, individual and group spiritual direction, days of recollection, retreats, conferences with mentors and program directors, and shared prayer and faith sharing as part of every program session. A second element is theological content, the depth and breadth of which will vary according to the responsibilities for which one is preparing. A third element is the development of ministerial skills, to be assessed by a supervised field experience. A fourth element includes the specialized knowledge and skills required by the particular ministry for which one is preparing.

Kinds of Preparation Programs

There are several kinds of programs that prepare lay ecclesial ministers; four types are distinct enough to enumerate:

(1) Diocesan formation programs that are multi-year programs and offer certificates or some other sign of successful completion
(2) Diocesan formation programs that are affiliated with a college, university, or seminary and offer certificates and degrees, sometimes through distance education
(3) Academic programs at institutions that offer certificates, undergraduate and graduate degrees, and some formation
(4) Non-degree programs sponsored by independent Catholic organizations

Five nationwide surveys of lay ministry formation programs have been conducted, first by the NCCB Committee on the Laity, and since 1994, by the Center for Applied Research in the Apostolate (CARA). In recent years, there has been a significant growth in the number of programs and students preparing for lay ministry. In 1986, there were 124 diocesan programs and 82 academic programs. The total enrollment in these programs was 10,500. By 1998, there were 183 programs sponsored by a diocese or archdiocese and 96 programs sponsored by a Catholic university or college. Of the diocesan-sponsored programs, 11 were affiliated with a seminary and 95 with a college or university. Independent Catholic organizations sponsor 10 other programs. In 1998, the total enrollment of these programs was 29,137. The majority of the students have always been women, although that percentage has declined slightly, from 65 percent in 1996 to 61 percent in 1998.

Lay ministry formation programs are conducted in a variety of languages. In 1998, of the 287 programs reporting the language they used, 229 used English only, 41 used English and Spanish, and 12 used Spanish only. Other languages included American Sign Language, Portuguese, and Navajo.

The *Catholic Ministry Formation Directory* (CARA, Bryan T. Froehle, ed., Washington, D.C.: Georgetown University Press, 1999) gives basic information about each of the programs, including sponsorship, accreditation, recognition or degrees granted, duration, where and when held, language(s) used, admission requirements, annual cost to student, and student profile.

Diocesan Formation Programs

The ways in which dioceses provide for the preparation of lay ministers vary widely and are affected by several factors, including the priorities and needs of the diocese, the prevailing ecclesiology, and the resources available within the diocese.

Most dioceses sponsor their own "free-standing" ministry formation programs. These programs, which can include catechesis, adult religious education, and faith formation, generally offer foundational theological content, formation experiences, and special tracks for particular ministries (such as youth ministers, family life ministers, and social outreach workers). These tracks often include supervised field experiences. Most of these programs require a commitment of three years and take place at several sites within the diocese, although some of them are given at a single site. All of them have some kind of admissions requirements and process.

In those cases where the diocese co-sponsors a program with a seminary, college, or university, the relationships are as unique as the diocese. In some cases, students go to campuses for classes; in other cases, faculty travel to off-campus sites within or even outside the diocese; in still other cases, videos of faculty are supplemented by local discussion leaders. An example of the latter is the extension program of Loyola University of New Orleans (LIMEX), which offers its programs in more than fifty dioceses throughout the United States. Students in this program may earn continuing education units, a master's degree in religious education or pastoral studies, or a certificate of advanced studies in pastoral life and administration.

At least two dioceses have certification processes that rely on local Catholic academic institutions, colleges, seminaries, and universities, rather than on a separate diocesan formation program. The portfolios of prospective ministers are reviewed by the diocese against a list of core academic competencies (Scripture, systematic theology, moral theology, liturgical and sacramental theology, pastoral/ministerial skills), and programs or courses are recommended. Candidates for certification meet regularly for formation and integration sessions, work with an experienced pastoral minister as mentor, and complete supervised field experiences.

Formation Programs in Spanish

According to research completed in 1999 by the Life Cycle Institute and Puentes, Inc., for the NCCB Committee on Hispanic Affairs, "formation programs for the laity are a major growth area in Hispanic Ministry." Separate bilingual or Spanish lay leadership programs exist in nearly 50 percent of the dioceses responding to their survey. The report distinguishes between two types of programs. One is the ongoing faith formation through catechesis and other programs, including marriage encounter and parish youth ministry. The other, more pertinent to our project, prepares leaders in areas such as liturgy, youth ministry, and the development of small faith communities. The leadership given by regional centers such as the Mexican American Cultural Center, the Southeast Pastoral Institute, and the Northeast Pastoral Formation Institute has given impetus and direction to the growth in diocesan and parish programs.

The Federation of Pastoral Institutes (Federación de Institutos Pastorales [FIP]) was formed in 1985 at the initiative of the Mexican American Cultural Center and the Southeast Pastoral Institute in order to design a common vision of formation, to create a system of collaboration, and to enrich one another by sharing experiences. The federation currently includes twenty-three member institutes, some of them serving several dioceses. It meets annually and has published the *Bilingual Manual Guide* and *Concepts and Practical Instruments for Pastoral Institutes*.

Financing the Preparation of Lay Ministers

A recent and slowly growing approach to the preparation of lay ministers, particularly for prospective pastoral associates and parish administrators, has been the practice of some dioceses to "sponsor" a student at one of the graduate schools for ministry. Several graduate schools have also taken the initiative of providing full or partial tuition scholarships for ministry students.

The financing of the preparation for lay ministers is one of the challenges facing the Church today. It is particularly acute among those communities that are poorer in economic resources, where prospective candidates for ministry frequently have greater educational needs.

Graduate Programs in Ministry

The Association of Graduate Programs in Ministry (AGPIM) was founded in 1987 as an organization of Roman Catholic graduate programs whose focus is the preparation of lay persons for ministry. According to AGPIM's mission statement, its goal is "to promote the quality of ministerial education in the service of church and society," and the association was founded "because of the burgeoning growth and significance of graduate ministry programs." The number of programs has grown from 82 in 1987 to 104 in 1999.

Representatives from AGPIM, like representatives from other ministerial associations, have been in dialogue with the lay ministry subcommittee throughout the project. One such dialogue included bishops, diocesan personnel responsible for staffing parishes, and representatives from the formation committees of the National Association for Lay Ministry (NALM) and AGPIM. Issues mentioned during that dialogue included the following, the first four of which had also been mentioned during the theological colloquium:

◆ Concern about the financing of ministry education for lay students
◆ Challenges of educating seminarians and lay ministry students together (desirable as a preparation for the practice of collaborative ministry, this sometimes raises concerns about maintaining priestly identity)
◆ Necessity of providing culturally appropriate formation programs for different cultural groups
◆ Necessity of preparing for the whole Church both ordained and lay ministers who are aware and affirming of all cultures
◆ Hope that dioceses might help the graduate schools with spiritual formation and related screening

USCC Commission on Certification and Accreditation

As its name indicates, the CCA is authorized to perform two functions: to accredit pastoral education programs that prepare persons for ministry in the Catholic Church and to approve certification standards of national organizations for specialized ministers and diocesan procedures for certification. The work that the commission does today began in 1962 when the National Catholic Welfare Conference (NCWC), in response to the need to certify Catholic chaplains for health care institutions, established the Board of Examiners and gave it responsibility for the certification of chaplains and the accreditation of training institutions.

According to the commission's current directory, there are thirty-three accredited programs, twenty-five of which are Clinical Pastoral Education (CPE) programs; the other eight are diocesan or academic formation programs. There are an additional twelve programs preparing for USCC accreditation, all but one of them diocesan or academic formation programs.

As a second part of its responsibility, the commission approves the certification standards of national organizations for specialized ministers, as well as diocesan certification procedures, based on those standards, for specialized ministers who are to be certified in the name of the United States Catholic Conference. The commission itself does not confer certification. The commission's directory lists six national organizations with approved standards and procedures for certifying specialized ministers, all of whom are chaplains—for airports, campuses, health care, prisons, seaports, and veterans affairs. It also lists three national organizations with approved standards for certifying specialized ministers: the National Association for Lay Ministry, which has standards for pastoral ministers, pastoral associates, and parish life coordinators; the National Conference of Catechetical Leaders (NCCL), which has standards for directors of religious education; and the National Federation of Catholic Youth Ministers (NFCYM), which has standards for youth ministers. Four diocesan offices have USCC-approved procedures for certifying specialized ministers.

Degrees, Credentials, Standards, and Certification

Church documents call for appropriate preparation of all who minister in the Church. While there are norms for the preparation of priests and deacons, there are none for lay ministers. The concern for appropriate preparation of all church ministers and the U.S. emphasis on professionalization and certification have impacted lay ecclesial ministry in a variety of ways. In some communities, credentialling is resisted, seen as merely academic or professional, qualities that are viewed as distinct from, if not in contradiction with, pastoral. In other communities, individuals are expected to complete many programs but are not given any credentials to carry with them.

The CCA-approved standards of three ministerial associations (NALM, NCCL, and NFCYM) are written as statements of competencies or descriptions of demonstrated behaviors that are organized as personal, theological, and professional. The three associations are preparing to publish a book that gives the background for these competencies and lists those competencies common to all the ministerial roles.

The attempt to create competency standards and a certification process for lay ministers in parish-level positions is still relatively new and, for that reason, not yet widely understood. Nonetheless, it has generated a great deal of interest and activity on the part of certain professional organizations as well as diocesan and university-based formation programs. The movement and energy is almost entirely a "bottom up" phenomenon. As is the case with other aspects of lay ministry, this is an example of a field gradually structuring itself. It is also significant that recognized standards now exist for those pastoral ministers, who considered together constitute the majority of the "new parish ministers." As such, this is a major movement of self-definition and accountability.

The development of "national standards" for certain ministries also, at least in theory, leads to the possibility of a person moving from one diocese to another and carrying with her or him a portfolio or credential that could be recognized in the new locale. This portability dimension, of course, depends on the widespread recognition by individual dioceses of the validity and necessity for certification.

Diocesan Certification Processes

A factor in making all this work effectively is whether and to what extent the bishops acknowledge and support what is occurring. It is possible that a diocesan office acting in the name of the bishop could be responsible for deciding what standards will be used and administering a certification process. This is the case in several dioceses and presumes a fairly well-articulated relationship (including a level of trust) between diocesan offices and parishes when it comes to taking responsibility for lay ecclesial ministers.

Recent research (*Parishes and Parish Ministers*, 1999) indicates that parish lay ministers experience more involvement from the diocese than they did five years ago. In 1992, 9.5 percent of lay ministers responded that the diocese had screened or certified them. In 1997, 35 percent were screened and 40 percent were certified. In 1992, 11 percent reported that the diocese had "established policies, ministry classifications, salary ranges"; in 1997, that percentage was 72 percent. In 1992, 8 percent reported that they were included in diocesan events; in 1997, that percentage was 83 percent. The ways in which such "inclusion" represents structured incorporation into the ministerial life of the diocese varies from diocese to diocese.

One tension point that might be anticipated in the use of competency-based certification for lay ministers is the difference between the expectations that are—or could be—in place for priests, deacons, and lay ministers. A tension point that has already been experienced occasionally occurs when a newly ordained associate pastor, prepared as a "generalist," arrives at a parish and must be integrated into a staff of specialists.

The Path to Lay Ministry

According to *Parishes and Parish Ministers*, engagement in parish ministry is a mixture of vocation—a call from God, invitation—by the pastor or other member of the parish staff, and attraction to the ministry itself—the varieties of ways to serve the parish community. *Called and Gifted for the Third Millennium* states that "ecclesial lay ministers speak of their work, their service, as a calling, not merely a job. They believe God has called them to their ministry, and often the parish priest is the means of discerning the call" (p. 17). The third edition of the NCCB *Guidelines for Diocesan Vocation Offices* (Washington, D.C.: United States Catholic Conference, 1998), adopted in November 1998, acknowledges the difficulty of using terms with precision because of "the developing sense of vocation and ministry" (p. 1). The Guidelines limit the word "vocation" to the "restricted sense of vocations to the priesthood, either religious or diocesan, and consecrated life" (p. 1). The experience of the subcommittee in listening to the stories of lay ministers themselves, their strong sense of vocation, and the sacrifices they and their families are willing to make in order for them to be faithful to that call suggests the need for further reflection on how the word "vocation" is used. Even if the definition of vocation were expanded to include all those called to the service of the Church—ordained, consecrated, lay—such expansion would still limit its use and make it difficult to appreciate the universal call to holiness (the vocation of every Christian that is lived out in a wide variety of specific ways). There clearly is a need to develop a more comprehensive theology of vocation.

Slightly more than half of the parish ministers who were studied in *Parishes and Parish Ministers* had been parishioners in the parish where they first became paid ministers, and almost half had been volunteering in the parish before they became a paid minister. The attraction to serving the parish community in specific or generic ways that leads to volunteering is an important element in the discernment of laity who subsequently become part of parish staffs.

In the same study, 87 percent of the pastors reported that they regularly or often turned to people they already knew when looking for a parish minister. Pastors rank good relational skills as the most important criterion for a parish minister.

The path to lay ecclesial ministry always begins with the inspiration of God. That inspiration is affirmed by the community, usually through its pastor, staff, or other leaders. The person sets out to acquire or develop the personal habits of mind and heart as well as the necessary learning and skills. This journey can involve participation in a diocesan ministry formation program and then graduate study. Those who experience a call to ministry when they are undergraduates and often involved in campus ministry, and who then go directly for graduate studies, can find their lack of parish ties to be a challenge as they try to find a place for ministry. The details of the path are as unique as the individuals themselves. Whatever the details, their paths deserve the encouragement and support, prayerful and practical, of the whole Church.

Improvements in Educational Preparation

Parishes and Parish Ministers also reports that the educational preparation of lay parish ministers has improved over the last five years. In 1992, 38.2 percent of full-time lay ministers had a master's degree or better; in 1997 that figure was 47.6 percent. This increase has occurred despite the declining number of vowed religious lay ministers who are generally more likely to have a graduate degree than other lay ministers. In 1997, 53.5 percent of all parish ministers, religious and lay, part-time and full-time, had at least a master's degree.

Research by the National Association of Parish Catechetical Directors reports that 58 percent of their members had master's degrees and 2 percent held doctorates. They also report that 11 percent did not have an academic degree in 1998, compared with 9 percent in 1992. Research by the National Conference of Catechetical Directors reports that 83 percent of diocesan directors of religious education held master's degrees and 13 percent held doctorates, percentages which have not changed since their 1989 study.

No research has focused on the number of ministers who have been certified through competency-based standards that measure pastoral and ministerial skills as well as theoretical knowledge. Such research as well as follow-up studies of those who complete diocesan and/or graduate ministry programs would be helpful for providing a more complete understanding of the current state of the preparation of lay ministers.

B. What We Learned from Bishops' Surveys and Focus Groups

The preparation of lay ecclesial ministers was a priority of the bishops who responded to the survey that initiated this project. Several bishops commented on the possibility of some kind of national or NCCB certification that could be recognized in every diocese. Others asked for more information about types of preparatory programs. The issue of preparation was also a high priority for dioceses, graduate schools, and ministerial associations. Their comments clustered around certification procedures and how best to ensure that the education and preparation included consideration of the experience of Christian living, integration into the ecclesial community, and apostolic and missionary witness.

The bishops' focus groups also discussed the preparation of lay ministers. Among their comments were the following:

- ◆ A very wide variety of approaches to preparation and certification is used across the country.
- ◆ Often a preference exists for identifying a prospective minister and then helping that person receive the necessary preparation,

rather than trying to evaluate the credentials, personal gifts, and biases that an already prepared person might bring to a parish or diocese.

◆ It is not too important to have national standards, according to one focus group member, "since most ministers stay within their dioceses, and there is enormous diversity across the country."

◆ Integration during the formation and education of priests and laity is key but very often challenging.

◆ A hope exists that the NCCB will develop national guidelines for the preparation of lay ministers: guidelines that could be a resource, not a strict requirement, for the dioceses.

C. What We Learned from Subcommittee Activities

The extensive subcommittee findings (pp. 28-39) were developed by staff-level research prompted by subcommittee discussions and activities.

The subcommittee has met with several groups and individuals who are concerned with the preparation of lay ministers. Before this project was funded by the Lilly Endowment, the subcommittee met with leaders of NALM for a discussion of the preparation of lay ministers. In addition, the subcommittee has held meetings with the executive director of the CCA and with the current and past presidents of AGPIM. Three bishops from the subcommittee and three additional diocesan bishops met with representatives from the formation committees of NALM and AGPIM for a one-day dialogue on the preparation of lay ministers.

Subcommittee members and project staff have participated in the annual meetings of NALM, and a member of the subcommittee serves as the episcopal liaison to NALM. Project staff have also participated in the annual meetings of AGPIM. The project coordinator serves as an advisor to the NALM formation committee and participates in the meetings of the three organizations (NALM, NCCL, and NFCYM) that are co-sponsoring the publication of a book on the competencies common among them as standards for their respective ministries. Project staff have also collaborated with CARA in the publication of the *Catholic Ministry Formation Directory*. The 1997-1998 directory was the first to include in a single volume information about seminaries and diaconate formation programs as well as lay ministry formation programs. Project staff assisted CARA staff by helping with the initial organization of the directory and reviewing survey instruments and preliminary results.

The Relationship Between Lay Ecclesial Ministers and Ordained Ministers

I. CONCLUSIONS AND PROPOSALS FROM THE SUBCOMMITTEE

CONCLUSION 1: The relationship of the bishop to the lay ecclesial minister needs further attention and clarification. That relationship needs to be expressed in rituals of installation and commissioning as well as in the administrative structures of the diocese.

CONCLUSION 2: It is essential to maintain the distinction between those ecclesial ministries that are entrusted to the laity appropriately because of their baptismal call and those ministries, ordinarily reserved to the ordained, which are delegated to the laity by exception in case of need. That distinction should be recognized in the titles, rituals, and canonical and liturgical forms used for the installation of all ecclesial ministers.

CONCLUSION 3: A wide variety of titles is used throughout the country for lay ministers, especially those lay ministers who are appointed under the provisions of canon 517.2 and those who are appointed to roles as "general pastoral ministers." Most dioceses have developed a schema for the use of such titles within the diocese. The November 1997 interdicasterial instruction, *Instruction on Certain Questions Regarding the Collaboration of the*

Non-Ordained Faithful in the Sacred Ministry of Priests (Washington, D.C.: United States Catholic Conference, 1998), emphasized the need for an appropriate terminology (article 1). The report of the Ad Hoc Committee on the Interdicasterial Instruction, citing such titles as "parish leader," "parish life coordinator," "parish moderator," and "parish administrator," stated that "these titles need further reflection in light of the recent instruction." The NCCB is already responding to this statement.

CONCLUSION 4: The appropriate incorporation of lay ecclesial ministers within the consultative structures of the diocese, particularly those lay ministers who are also parish life coordinators (appointed according to canon 517.2) or general pastoral ministers, is necessary. A few models are currently in use, some of them recently developed.

CONCLUSION 5: A concern exists on the part of some that giving attention to lay ecclesial ministry will detract from attention to encouraging vocations to the ordained priesthood. We believe this concern should be acknowledged and addressed in a way that honors the essential role of the ordained priesthood and the complementary roles of lay ecclesial ministers.

PROPOSALS TO BE CONSIDERED BY BISHOPS

(1) That the conference continue to study the relationship between the bishop and the lay ecclesial minister and that relationship's theological and practical implications.

(2) That the conference research and prepare guidelines, which could be adapted by individual dioceses, for (a) existing practices for installation and commissioning and (b) the various titles and descriptions used throughout

the country for lay ministry positions. This proposal would help diocesan staff develop their own titles and descriptions.

II. BACKGROUND FOR SUBCOMMITTEE CONCLUSIONS AND PROPOSALS

A. Subcommittee Findings

This issue can be seen both as a theological issue and as one that has organizational and interpersonal dimensions.

Theological Dimensions

The relationship of the lay ecclesial minister to the bishop emerged as one of the central themes in subcommittee discussions. It is a relationship desired by the lay ministers themselves as an expression of their role within the local church. There is also a concern that, on occasion, some lay ministers develop and minister from a too parochial view of the church. The nature of this relationship of the bishop with the lay ecclesial ministers—its theological and practical implications—is one that requires further exploration and attention. How this relationship is expressed and ritualized is another issue that needs attention. There is widespread concern about the current use of the word "commissioning" to signify the completion of a program of study and supervised experiences, instead of its proper use to signify the beginning of an appointment to a specific ministry assignment.

Lay Ministers in the Organizational Setting

Parishes and Parish Ministers reports that parishes are becoming more structured with regard to all these matters (clarity of position and responsibility, salary or stipend, working relationships with the pastor and other staff, and material resources for the work). They are moving "from a rather familial style . . . to a more organizational one" (p. 55). The fact that diocesan involvement in some of these areas has increased may account for some of the change. Parish ministers report almost unanimously that their roles have been sufficiently structured and that they have been given sufficient authority to carry out their ministry. The report also indicates that relationships are fine in all but about 10 to 15 percent of the parishes.

In all of this, it is important to repeat a caution from the report: "Remember, most parishes have only one [lay] parish minister and, as long as the communication is good, it is likely that the division of labor will require the pastor and the parish minister to work on their own with the parishioners" (p. 57).

This research also examines the general model of the parish staff. Here the perceptions of the parish ministers differ from those of the pastor: 58 percent of the pastors see the staff relationship as collaborative rather than independent, but only 31 percent of the parish ministers see it that way. Similarly, 50 percent of the pastors see the staff relationship as team rather than staff, but only 35 percent of the parish ministers see it that way.

B. What We Learned from Bishops' Surveys and Focus Groups

Again, this issue of the relationship between lay ecclesial ministers and ordained ministers was seen both as a theological issue and as one with organizational and interpersonal dimensions. The item that the bishops were asked to prioritize in their survey instrument was "fostering improved relationships between priests and lay ministers." The bishops' suggestions on this item included "introducing [first time] lay ministers," "reintroducing a pastor in parishes that have had a pastoral coordinator," "prepar[ing] and educat[ing] our priests for greater involvement of the laity," and "helping priests assume the responsibility and, if possible, the role of 'formator' of volunteer lay ministers in a parish." In addition to the suggestions, the bishops also had questions: "How does the priest exercise his spiritual leadership vis-à-vis lay ministers?" and "How do we convince our people (perhaps priests) that lay ministry is not second-class ministry but a responsibility flowing from baptism?"

In two separate focus groups, the relationship issue was broadened to include deacons as a distinct category to be considered in the relationship question. Another group emphasized the need for better seminary training, helping prospective priests develop leadership skills for coordinating staffs in addition to pastoral counseling skills for working with individuals. One group commented that the issue is leadership development, not collaboration. In another group, the discussion of the role of the priest as enabler/coordinator led to the request for improving working relationships between priests and lay ministers by providing better training for both groups. Group members noted that lay ministry should not be seen as being in competition with recruiting priests. That group also identified the difference between the priest's commitment to the diocese and what is perceived as the lay minister's freedom to leave at any time as a cause of tension in some relationships.

C. What We Learned from Subcommittee Activities

During the first year of the project, the subcommittee engaged in a "structured conversation" led by Msgr. Murnion on the relationship between ordained and lay ministers. The discussion, which continued throughout two subcommittee meetings, included references to the many workshops on collaboration already available for those preparing for or engaged in ministry.

The theological dimensions of the issue were among those treated during the discussions at the theological colloquium. They were highlighted by the interdicasterial instruction, *Instruction on Certain Questions Regarding the Collaboration of the Non-Ordained Faithful in the Sacred Ministry of Priests*. The committee formed to study the instruction was chaired by one of the bishops of the Subcommittee on Lay Ministry with three other bishops from the subcommittee among its members.

Consultations have occurred with diocesan priests in three different parts of the country, with the priest consultors to the NCCB Committee on Priestly Life and Ministry, and with the board of the National Association of Diaconate Directors. Project staff have also been in frequent dialogue with staff from the NCCB offices for priestly life and ministry, priestly formation, and the diaconate. Those consultations have affirmed our conviction that clarity of roles and definitions are desired and needed by all church ministers. They have also shown that some priests do not believe that establishing an on-going relationship between bishops and lay ministers is as important as some bishops and lay ministers themselves have indicated.

Financial and
Human Resources Issues

I. CONCLUSIONS AND PROPOSAL FROM THE SUBCOMMITTEE

CONCLUSION 1: *Parishes and Parish Ministers* contains evidence of the increasing use of formal job descriptions and contracts, performance evaluations, and staff meetings. We believe that these standard human resources practices will enhance lay ecclesial ministry, and we encourage their further development.

CONCLUSION 2: While salaries for lay ecclesial ministers have improved in the last five years and the majority of lay ministers report satisfaction with their salaries, income level is the factor they most often cite as needing improvement and as causing them to go on to other employment. Lay ministers also need support for continuing education and retreats. We encourage dioceses and parishes to address creatively the issue of just compensation, which includes both salaries and benefits for lay ecclesial ministers, and at the same time, to recognize appropriately those who serve in similar roles without compensation.

CONCLUSION 3: Grievance procedures and due process are essential to the just treatment of all workers. As the composition of the "work force" of the Church changes to include increasing numbers of lay persons, these persons become particularly important. To those dioceses who are developing or revising such procedures, we recommend consultation with experts such as staff of the National Association of Church Personnel Administrators (NACPA).

CONCLUSION 4: Given the mobility that characterizes our society, the portability of pension benefits is a legitimate concern of lay ecclesial ministers. That concern is most effectively addressed by groups of dioceses or by the NCCB itself.

CONCLUSION 5: Stable employment is another legitimate concern of lay ecclesial ministers. We recognize that changes in parish leadership can be fruitful for all parishes, but we recommend that dioceses develop policies that will ensure just procedures for all employed by the parish—procedures that guarantee that policy and not personal biases determine continued employment or termination. It is encouraging to see instances in which dioceses give assistance to those terminated in good standing in order to help them find new placements.

CONCLUSION 6: The clergy, religious, and lay who serve together within one diocese, church institution, or national office constitute in those settings a single ministerial body. Each group has challenges and needs specific to its state in life and ministry focus. We support the development of comprehensive, integrated personnel systems. "Comprehensiveness does not seek to apply the same policy to all groups, but rather to create consistent policies, coming from the same basic philosophical stance, which take into consideration the needs of all three groups, and, indeed, the interests of the entire church" (NACPA, *The Individual and the Institution: Strengthening Working Relationships in the Church*, Cincinnati, Ohio: NACPA, 1994, p. 10).

PROPOSAL TO BE CONSIDERED BY BISHOPS

That the conference explore models of portable pension benefits, including those similar to the plans offered to individuals in higher education, that could be adapted for lay ministers at the national level. Dioceses would have the option of participating in such a plan.

II. BACKGROUND FOR SUBCOMMITTEE CONCLUSIONS AND PROPOSAL

A. Subcommittee Findings

There is a clear need for attention to these issues, but it is questionable how much of that attention can be directed from a national level. The Church already has a long and honored list of statements that call for the just treatment of all workers. The 1971 Synod of Bishops, for example, called upon the Church itself to look internally and examine how it acts justly: "While the Church is bound to give witness to justice, she recognizes that anyone who ventures to speak to people about justice must first be just in their eyes" (*Justice in the World*, III, 40). The implementation of those statements must, for the most part, be carried out at a diocesan and parish level.

NACPA already provides valued services and resources to many dioceses and parishes. Their suggestion is that there be one human resources staff person for every 100 employees. Dioceses should have someone on staff to help parishes, especially with issues of placement, termination, and supervision. NACPA surveys indicate that provision of opportunities for continuing education; retreat and spiritual direction time; and training in leadership, supervisory skills, and team building are important to lay ministers. Surveys also reported that only 40 percent of workers within the Church expect to receive just treatment. NACPA notes that working within the Church is often perceived as working within a "flat" system with few opportunities for advancement, even though the position itself offers opportunities for growth. The younger a person is, the less likely he/she expects to be able to work in the Church for the long term. The issue of portability of credentials and benefits is an important one for lay ministers.

Parishes and Parish Ministers reports that salaries for lay ministers improved in real dollars from 1992 to 1997 and that the majority are satisfied with their salaries, agreeing that their salaries are adequate to their needs. More than one-quarter of all parish ministers and one-third of those who find their salaries inadequate think that the parish can't afford an adequate salary. The income level is the factor most cited as needing improvement and the reason most cited as possibly causing parish ministers to seek other employment.

The study also reports that parish ministry is extremely satisfying. Lay ministers note that they have grown closer to God, to the Church, and to the parish. "[They] know the importance of the service they provide, find their situation an immensely rewarding one, and feel very much appreciated for what they are doing" (p. 63). That satisfaction is evident in the intention of four out of five of the parish ministers planning to remain in the ministry for the foreseeable future.

B. What We Learned from Bishops' Surveys and Focus Groups

Bishops responding to the survey identified several specific financial and human resources issues in their comments. One bishop noted that "funding for lay ministry is very important, especially in poorer dioceses." Another cited the problem of "letting a lay minister go for good reason, but without being able to offer him/her any other position—knowing that the minister has family responsibilities." Other comments identified the challenge of dealing with the high rate of turnover among lay ministers. One diocesan response asked how lay ministry can be a more realistic option for qualified and dedicated lay persons who are supporting families. Another asked about educating parish pastoral councils in the ethical considerations for the hiring process and for the compensation package. Another bishop asked about the ethical human resources considerations for terminating lay ecclesial ministers.

During the focus groups, bishops also discussed several aspects of the issues. One group shared their experiences of "at will" employment as distinct from the use of contracts, noting the bishop's responsibility to protect the diocese as much as possible from law suits. Almost every group mentioned the challenges that accompany the appointment of a new pastor and the adjustments that appointment brings to parish staffing. One group commented on the role that the diocese should play in the hiring process by establishing criteria but not doing the actual hiring. Several mentioned the challenge of appointing an ordained pastor to a parish that had previously had a lay pastoral coordinator. One group mentioned the low level of giving in Catholic parishes and the need for educating parishioners. Another group commented on the impact on family life of ecclesial ministry, which takes place mostly in the evenings and on weekends. At least two groups noted that although these issues are very important, the project needs to give primary attention to the theological and ministerial issues. Greater clarification and understanding of the latter will facilitate dealing with the former set of issues.

C. What We Learned from Subcommittee Activities

At one of its first meetings in November 1996, the subcommittee met with staff of NACPA. The two forums for representatives of professional associations, while not specifically focused on human resources issues, inevitably touched on many of them as the lay ministers themselves shared their experiences. The regular updates on the research for *Parishes and Parish Ministers*, which Msgr. Murnion gave at each subcommittee meeting, kept the subcommittee informed about developments in this area.

Project staff have participated in and reported on the project at the annual "Convening on Just Treatment for Those Who Work for the Church," which NACPA sponsors for representatives of national organizations. Project staff have also participated in the annual NACPA convocation.

Multicultural Issues

I. CONCLUSIONS AND PROPOSAL FROM THE SUBCOMMITTEE

CONCLUSION 1: Most ethnic and cultural communities are not proportionately represented among the employed lay ecclesial ministers. Some members of these communities are recent arrivals in this country, and many, though not all, are poor. All of these communities have rich traditions to offer the Church and call forth leaders from within their own communities. We believe that greater numbers of lay ecclesial ministers should be drawn from the communities they serve. (Note: Data to support this conclusion [definitions and percentages] are inconsistent, shifting from one source to another. The chart below includes data published by *Parishes and Parish Ministers*; James D. Davidson, et al., *The Search for Common Ground: What Unites and Divides Catholic Americans* [Huntington, Ind.: Our Sunday Visitor, 1997]; and the *Catholic Ministry Formation Directory 1999*.

Percentages of U.S. Catholics, Lay Ecclesial Ministers, and Lay Ministry Students

	Catholics in U.S. Population	Lay Ecclesial Ministers	Lay Ministry Students
Hispanic Americans	13-40%	4.4%	23%
African Americans	3-5%	1.2%	3%
Asian Americans	>2%	0.6%	2%
American Indians	<1%	0.1%	1%

CONCLUSION 2: Our Church is impoverished when the gifts of all are not available to all or not nurtured for the wider Church. We believe the NCCB should explore the development of policies and strategies to identify, support, and properly prepare lay ministers who come from all the cultural groups within our Church and who are ready to serve not only within their own communities but within the wider Church.

CONCLUSION 3: The ethnic and cultural diversity of the Church within the United States requires that all ministry training be done with an awareness of the many cultural contexts within our Church. We believe that it is necessary to prepare all ministers for the whole Church, aware and affirming of all cultures.

PROPOSAL TO BE CONSIDERED BY BISHOPS

That the conference continue to convene key individuals and groups who together can study and identify ways to recognize, support, and properly prepare lay ministers from those parts of the Church that are underserved and underrepresented among lay ecclesial ministers.

II. BACKGROUND FOR SUBCOMMITTEE CONCLUSIONS AND PROPOSAL

A. Subcommittee Findings

Multicultural issues are complex, changing, and challenging. The complexity is compounded by the wide varieties and definitions of culture and ethnicity that are part of our contemporary Church in the United States. *The General Directory for Catechesis* (Washington, D.C.: United States Catholic Conference, 1997) speaks of the process required for inculturation of the faith as "a profound and global process and a slow journey" (no. 109). In a country such as ours, which boasts of so many cultures, that process and journey will inevitably be even more profound and slow. The growth and immigration patterns of our U.S. population, the changing locations of different groups (urban/suburban, southwest/northeast) within the country, the upward economic mobility of some immigrant groups, the shifting positions of dominant and minority groups, and other such factors present to the Church challenges that change almost from year to year. All of these issues must be addressed by the Church. While we addressed multicultural issues directly, we also used them as a lens to consider the other issues; accordingly, some of our findings have been incorporated in earlier sections of our report when they were specifically tied to the issue under discussion there (see pp. 31-32).

Within the so-called minority communities, ministry is clearly seen as service to the community, but rarely is it recognized as a profession or career. The bulk of the work is done by volunteers—volunteers who see a need and respond or who are called by their pastor to meet a need. As natural gifts are recognized and called forth by the community, training is sometimes given through workshops and weekend sessions. Many participate in whatever formation programs are available. Often training and formation opportunities are offered to those representing the dominant population first and then to others only if funds are still available.

We learned that leadership is identified, developed, exercised, and accepted in different ways in different cultural groups. Charismatic rather than credentialed leadership is important in many minority communities. Recognition by the community for experience, wisdom, and holiness is sometimes seen as more essential than professional training. Ministerial expertise is gained in the field more than in the classroom. Leadership is seen as a personal relationship, and its development is a very gradual process. According to a participant at one forum, the process can be frustrated by the time lines, flow charts, and goals and objectives statements that are a part of the dominant culture. At the same time, we learned that members of minority communities often feel that they are not given adequate resources for training and education and that when their leaders are prepared, they are not considered for leadership beyond their own community.

We learned that dioceses and many academic institutions take seriously their responsibility to prepare individuals from diverse cultural groups for lay ecclesial ministry. The sixty-two ministry formation programs that use Spanish and the twenty-three member institutes of the FIP are evidence that the Church is responding to the present and preparing for the future.

B. What We Learned from Bishops' Surveys and Focus Groups

Even though multicultural issues were addressed only obliquely in the survey, several bishops used the occasion to register concern about cultural and ethnic diversity within the Church. One wrote, "[I would like the project to address] theology of ministry and the formation and education of lay ministers from the African American and Hispanic communities." Another bishop noted that in his diocese "our population is 25 percent Hispanic, 25 percent Asian-Pacific Islander, and 25 percent foreign-born. Perceptions and expectations in those cultures will profoundly affect lay ministry in the U.S." Another bishop asked, "How do we attract minorities [to lay ecclesial ministry]?"

The focus groups also addressed the varieties of cultures within the Church, referring to the accomplishments and needs of the Native American, Hispanic, African American, and Asian American communities in different parts of the country.

C. What We Learned from Subcommittee Activities

Appointment of Additional Advisor

During the discussion of multicultural issues at the June 1996 sub-committee meeting, there was recognition of the need to have someone present who could bring that dimension to all discussion and planning. Dr. Zoila Diaz, academic dean at St. Vincent de Paul Regional Seminary in Boynton Beach, Fla., accepted the invitation to serve as an advisor to the subcommittee. At the March 1997 meeting, Dr. Diaz led a discussion on cultural diversity and its impli-cations for lay ministry, citing in particular the different ways lead-ership is exercised within the Spanish-speaking community and the constraints that economic hardships and family role expectations impose on those communities. She also shared the U.S. Census Bureau population projections for 2050, which show significant increases in the present minority populations.

Theological Colloquium

Participants at the May 1997 theological colloquium included rep-resentatives from the Hispanic and African American communities. During one of the general discussion sessions, Fr. Allan Figueroa Deck, SJ, mentioned the changing profile of the Catholic Church in the United States and the need to integrate those changes into all planning for lay ecclesial ministry.

Consultation with Ethnic Groups Representatives

In March 1997, the subcommittee met with seventeen representa-tives from ethnic communities for a day-long dialogue on lay eccle-sial ministry. The representatives, who had been identified by the NCCB/USCC staffs for the departments and secretariats of pastoral care of migrants and refugees, African American Catholics, Hispanic affairs, and education, came from the African American, Cambodian, Filipino, Guatemalan, Haitian, Korean, Mexican

American, Native American, Nigerian, and Puerto Rican communities. The representatives were lay and ordained; married, single, and religious. Many of them served in diocesan offices, others in higher education, and some in parishes. In small and large group sessions, the subcommittee learned about the great importance of volunteer ministers, different understandings and experiences of leadership, the need for resources, the isolation and marginalization experienced, the diversities within each community, and the strong sense that, as one speaker said, "ethnic lay leaders are for the entire Church, not just for their own communities." A major discovery was that the definition of lay ecclesial minister proposed by the subcommittee at that time was too restrictive, not acknowledging the gifts and alternate paths to ministry within the ethnic communities.

Continental Dialogue

In June 1998, the subcommittee hosted a two-day dialogue on lay ecclesial ministry that included five bishops from the Latin American Bishops' Council (CELAM) and a bishop and lay woman from the Canadian Conference of Catholic Bishops. The dialogue was focused on the common commitment of all the participants to fostering lay ministry within the Church, a commitment affected by very different cultural and ecclesial realities. Talking about the differences of a faith and Church brought by conquerors or immigrants, stability or mobility, poverty or middle class affluence, valuing of relationships and community or of individualism and independence led one subcommittee advisor to observe later that, in many ways, ministry is culture-specific. In South America, for example, lay ministry flourishes most in the rural areas and *barrios* where advanced study is not usually an option. The dominant culture in the United States, on the other hand, values formal education and organizational patterns of social life; professionalization and specialization is expanding in every area of work.

Lay Ministry Update

The newsletter *Lay Ministry Update*, which was distributed during the project to all bishops and 150 other ministry formation leaders, featured in each of its eighteen issues a regular section that reported on lay ministry in other countries.

Appendix 1: Subcommittee Proposals for Bishops' Consideration

These proposals are already contained throughout this report in the appropriate sections. They are gathered here for ease of reading.

General Proposal

That the conference establish a permanent place within its committee and staff structures to address the continuing development of lay ecclesial ministry.

Proposal on the Theology of Lay Ecclesial Ministry

That the conference make provision within its committee structure to continue to promote and to share the results of the following:

(1) Dialogue among bishops, theologians, canonists, ordained ministers, and lay ecclesial ministers for the further articulation of the theology of lay ecclesial ministry.

(2) Scholarly research and writing about the theology of ministry, including such aspects as ministry rooted in the sacraments of initiation as well as in the gifts of the Spirit, the relationship between baptism and orders, and the lay vocation to ministry.

Proposals on the Preparation of Lay Ministers

(1) That the conference offer guidance for the preparation of lay ecclesial ministers. That guidance would be developed from

existing resources (e.g., nationally approved standards) and experiences (diocesan ministry formation and graduate programs in ministry) and could be applied according to local situations and circumstances. The guidance could be in the form of a handbook similar to the directory being prepared for deacons, although it would not have the force of particular law.

(2) That the conference facilitate dialogue among the various institutions involved with the formation of lay ecclesial ministers, with the goal of ensuring the best use of resources and the provision of quality programs for prospective lay ministers.

Proposals on the Relationship Between Lay Ministers and Ordained Ministers

(1) That the conference continue to study the relationship between the bishop and the lay ecclesial minister and that relationship's theological and practical implications.

(2) That the conference research and prepare guidelines, which could be adapted by individual dioceses, for (a) existing practices for installation and commissioning and (b) the various titles and descriptions used throughout the country for lay ministry positions. This proposal would help diocesan staff develop their own titles and descriptions.

Proposal on Human Resources Issues

That the conference explore models of portable pension benefits, including those similar to the plans offered to individuals in higher education, that could be adapted for lay ministers at the national level. Dioceses would have the option of participating in such a plan.

Proposal on Multicultural Issues

That the conference continue to convene key individuals and groups who together can study and identify ways to recognize, support, and properly prepare lay ministers from those parts of the Church that are underserved and underrepresented among lay ecclesial ministers.

Appendix 2: Questions from the Subcommittee

A. Toward a Theology of Lay Ecclesial Ministry

◆ Do the conclusions of the subcommittee contain a sufficient analysis of the new reality and of relevant church teaching from which a theology of lay ecclesial ministry could be developed? If something else is required, what is it? Are there some elements that should be emphasized more than others?

◆ What are your concerns and hopes for developing a theological foundation for lay ecclesial ministry?

◆ What can the NCCB do in relation to this issue?

B. The Vocation of Lay Ecclesial Ministers

◆ How can bishops respond to the pervasive sense among lay ecclesial ministers that they are called to a distinct vocation within the Church?

◆ How can the conference encourage continued development of a theology of vocation, a theology grounded in the universal call to holiness that recognizes lay vocations to church ministry?

◆ How can the concern that giving attention to lay ecclesial ministry will detract from encouraging vocations to the ordained priesthood and consecrated life be addressed in a way that honors the essential role of the ordained priests and the complementary roles of lay ecclesial ministers?

◆ What are your concerns and hopes about this issue?

◆ What can the conference do in relation to this issue?

C. Formation and Preparation of Lay Ecclesial Ministers

♦ Should the NCCB offer guidance for the preparation of lay ecclesial ministers? The guidance would be developed from church teaching, theological and canonical sources, existing resources (e.g., nationally approved standards), and experiences (diocesan ministry formation and graduate ministry programs) and could be applied according to local situations and circumstances. The guidance could be in the form of a handbook similar to the directory being prepared for deacons, although it would not have the force of particular law.

♦ Are there other initiatives that the conference might undertake about the formation and preparation of lay ecclesial ministers, for example, providing information on models of preparation as well as on current credentialling, certification, and assessment criteria and processes?

♦ How might the conference assist dioceses in the development of plans for financing the preparation of lay ecclesial ministers, which would relieve some of the burden placed on the individual minister and allow poorer parishes to educate their leaders who often are minority group members?

♦ What are your concerns and hopes about this issue?

♦ What can the conference do in relation to this issue?

D. Relationship of Lay and Ordained Ministers

♦ Does the description offered for lay ecclesial ministers (pp. 7-8) help to advance our understanding of the distinction between as well as the complementary roles of lay ecclesial and ordained ministers and of the distinction between lay ecclesial ministers and other laity?

♦ What kinds of formation and continuing education opportunities promote better relationships between lay and ordained ministers?

- What are your concerns and hopes about this issue?
- What can the NCCB do in relation to this issue?

E. Lay Ecclesial Ministry in a Multicultural Church

- How might the conference assist in the development of policies and strategies to identify, support, and properly prepare lay ecclesial ministers for those parts of the Church that are currently underserved and underrepresented among the lay ecclesial ministers?
- What can be done to ensure that all ministers of the Church understand the whole Church as it is today and that all ministers are called to serve throughout the whole Church, that is, not confined to their own ethnic group?
- What are your concerns and hopes about this issue?
- What can the NCCB do in relation to this issue?

Appendix 3: Chronology of the NCCB Subcommittee on Lay Ministry

1994

March	Subcommittee established by the NCCB Committee on the Laity
June	Subcommittee expanded to include bishops from other ministry-related committees
November	Approval of proposal to Lilly Endowment for project entitled "Leadership for Lay Ecclesial Ministry"

1995

March	Discussion with Dr. Zeni Fox, advisor to the subcommittee, on how lay ecclesial ministry can be distinguished from lay ministry in general and what kinds of lay ministries can be included within the term; consultation with representatives of NALM and AGPIM; review and revision of proposal
June	Consultation with representatives from the University of Notre Dame about formation and continuing education of lay ecclesial ministers; discussion with representative from the Conference for Pastoral Planning and Council Development about parish restructuring, as well as expansion and diversification of lay ecclesial ministries

November   Announcement of funding of project by Lilly; consultation about trends in the formation and education of lay ecclesial ministers with representatives from the DeSales School of Theology and Education for Parish Service; introduction of interim project coordinator

1996

January   Beginning of Lilly-funded project "Leadership for Lay Ecclesial Ministry"; survey of bishops, dioceses, graduate programs in ministry, and lay ministerial associations; first issue of *Lay Ministry Update*, which is continued bimonthly

Spring   Five focus groups involving thirty-three bishops in different sections of the country

March   Forum with representatives of twenty-one professional associations and graduate programs in ministry; decision to sponsor a theological colloquium; distribution of survey results to all bishops; introduction of permanent project coordinator

June   Consultation with the executive director of the CCA about the work of the commission; discussion of the many facets of priest-lay minister relationships with Msgr. Murnion; decision to invite Zoila Diaz, D. Min., to serve as advisor to subcommittee

November   Consultation with representatives from NACPA

1997

March   Discussion of multicultural issues in lay ministry with Dr. Diaz; consultation on education and formation issues with representatives from AGPIM

May   Theological colloquium, "Toward a Theology of Ecclesial Lay Ministry," with approximately fifty bishops, theologians, and other experts in lay ministry participating

June   Review of colloquium consensus statements; development of a working paper on the theology of lay ecclesial ministry; decision to distribute colloquium papers to all bishops

September Forum with twenty-two representatives of nineteen national lay ministerial associations

November Workshop for bishops "The Bishop and Ecclesial Lay Ministry," with approximately seventy bishops participating; review and revision of working paper on theology of lay ministry; consultation with the USCC Office for Hispanic Affairs on meeting with ethnic representatives; decision to sponsor a continental dialogue on lay ministry

1998

March   Consultation with seventeen representatives of ten ethnic communities; review and revision of working paper on theology of lay ministry

June   "Continental Dialogue on Lay Ministry" with five bishops from CELAM and one bishop and lay woman from the Canadian Conference of Catholic Bishops; outline for proposed statement on lay ministry

August   Consultation on the preparation of lay ministers with six bishops, representatives from formation committees of NALM and AGPIM, and individuals responsible for staffing parishes; publication of *Together in God's Service: Toward a Theology of Ecclesial Lay Ministry* by the United States Catholic Conference

November Consultation with Sr. Bríd Long, SSL, on Lilly evaluation process; review of proposed statement on lay ministry; completion of project and announcement of Lilly grant for work through 1999; decision to prepare report for discussion rather than statement for a vote

1999

March	Consultation with Sr. Long, SSL, on Lilly evaluation report; review and revision of draft of report and process for discussion by bishops
May	Publication of *Parishes and Parish Ministers* by National Pastoral Life Center and distribution to all bishops; first consultation with priests
June	Review and revision of draft of reports and process for discussion by bishops; approval of plans to continue work through 2000
August	Consultation with priests
September	Consultations with priests and deacons
October	Consultation with priests
November	Presentation and discussion of report by U.S. bishops at general meeting; consideration of proposals for future activity

Appendix 4: Members of the NCCB Subcommittee on Lay Ministry

Most Reverend Phillip F. Straling
Chairman

Most Reverend Tod D. Brown
Former Chairman, Committee on the Laity

Most Reverend John C. Dunne
Former Member, Committee on Consecrated Life
Former Chairman, Committee on Women in Church and Society

Most Reverend Bernard J. Harrington
(1996-1997)
Member, Committee on Priestly Life and Ministry

Most Reverend James R. Hoffman
Member at large

Most Reverend Gerald F. Kicanas
Former Member, Committee on Priestly Formation
Chairman, Committee on the Diaconate

Most Reverend Edward U. Kmiec
Former Chairman, Committee on the Diaconate

Most Reverend Armando X. Ochoa
Member, Committee on the Diaconate

Most Reverend J. Terry Steib, SVD
(1994-1996)
Member, Committee on Priestly Life and Ministry

Most Reverend Emil A. Wcela
Former Member, Committee on Pastoral Practices

ADVISORS

Zoila Diaz, D. Min.
Academic Dean, St. Vincent de Paul Regional Seminary

Zeni Fox, Ph.D.
Associate Professor and Director of Lay Ministry,
Immaculate Conception Seminary

Monsignor Philip J. Murnion
Director, National Pastoral Life Center